101 U

for a
Flat Cap

written by
Ian McMillan
illustrated by
Tony Husband

Dalesman

First published in 2013 by Dalesman
an imprint of
Country Publications Ltd
The Water Mill, Broughton Hall
Skipton, North Yorkshire BD23 3AG
www.dalesman.co.uk

Text © Ian McMillan 2013
Cartoons © Tony Husband 2013

ISBN 978-1-85568-316-7

Printed in China by 1010 Printing International Ltd.

The nobility of the flat cap

By Professor Walt Blenkinsop of Heckmondwike University

The book you hold in your hand (unless you're just picking up from the floor because I startled you with my voice — sorry) is an attempt to restore the flat cap to its rightful place in the pantheon of the world's headgear.

Let's face it, the flat cap doesn't normally get a very good press. If any news organisation wants to show a story based in Yorkshire, they'll begin with sentimental brass band music and a shot of some old toothless chaps in caps. If a character in a play is given a comedy Yorkshire accent, the odds are that he'll be wearing a flat cap.

Well, here in Yorkshire we know differently. We know that the flat cap is not only a great cultural *objet d'art*, it's also a symbol of dignity and elevated philosophical thought. Think of it as a fedora with style, or a bowler hat with dignity.

Step into this book and read it, then step out of it at the end with pride in the glorious flat cap.

Averting a dam disaster

During the great Scissett Floods of 1836, Obadiah Smythe was walking the flooded fields searching for flotsam and jetsam. Truth to tell, Obadiah was a bit of a bad lad: he'd been up before the beak a few times for petty theft and for shouting 'Hoy!' in the street after 7pm. He was hoping to find things washed up in the flood that he could sell to his mates in the King's Head.

He wandered around to Marshfield Dam, which was holding back the floodwaters from the fertile valley below. He noticed, as he bent to pick up a farthing, that a hole was appearing, and widening, in the dam.

Obadiah tried to stick his finger in it, but the hole was too big; he had to think quickly. He whipped off his flat cap and stuck it in the hole. It held, just, and the valley was saved.

Obadiah was the hero of the day, and his statue can still be seen in the main square of Scissett.

Ten locations named after the flat cap

Flat Cap Hill, Illinois. Named after settlers from Leeds moved there in 1723.

Flat Cap Mountain, Illinois. Named after settlers from Bradford moved there in 1724. It's actually two miles from Flat Cap Hill and is really a hill.

Flat Cap City. Named by the aforementioned Leeds Settlers in 1725. It's a street at the foot of Flat Cap Hill.

Flat Cap Metropolis. Named by the Bradford settlers in 1726. It's two streets by the Flat Cap Lake.

Flat Cap Inland Ocean. A small lake near Flat Cap City named by the Leeds Settlers in 1727.

Flat Cap Moon. A controversial renaming of the Moon by the aforementioned Leeds settlers.

Flat Cap Sun. A controversial renaming of the Sun by the aforementioned Bradford settlers in 1728.

Flat Cap Universe. A controversial renaming of the Universe by the aforementioned Leeds settlers in 1729.

Flat Cap Everything That Ever Existed. A controversial renaming of Everything That Ever Existed by the aforementioned Bradford settlers in 1730.

Flat Cap Battlefield. Site of the infamous 1731 Flat Cap Battle.

CHRISTMAS CAPPERS

Dear Sir,

It might interest your readers to know that for the last 45 years our family has been pulling flat caps rather than Christmas crackers because we feel it is a more 'Yorkshire' thing to do.

We buy a supply of cheap caps from charity shops, form them into a cylinder and fill them with a joke, a paper flat cap (of course!) and a special Yorkshire prize like a Yorkshire Pudding Badge or a Novelty Parkin Jigsaw.

Imagine the hilarity at the Christmas party! Especially as they're rather hard to pull...

Yours in Yorkshireness

Betty Green

A letter in the *Heckmondwike Gazette*, 17th November 1992

CAPMAN

The tale of Ronald Mason, inventor-at-large

It's not too well known that in the last years of the Victorian era there was quite a fad for Inventing Competitions in newspapers and magazines.

Readers would be asked to invent some new device or machine, a shortlist of which would then be put up to the Patent Office at the publication's cost; if the invention was deemed good enough to be patented, the publication would share in any rewards. This method is how we got the Reversible Fork and the Flying Zip Scoop Bucket.

One week, readers of the *Skipton Trumpet* were asked to design a new Flat Cap, one that would retain all the features of the original but which would somehow improve on what was actually a classic piece of design.

Sadly the word Cap was misprinted as Cup, so it appeared that readers were being asked to create a new Flat Cup. Most readers realised the mistake and set about creating a new Flat Cap. Apart from

Ronald, who got his drawing board out and dreamed of the Flat Cup he would make.

He instantly hit a problem, of course, which is that a cup is concave for a reason: to hold the liquid in. A flat cap is flat.

Ronald eventually came up with a design that looked a bit like a mortar board with a handle. He reasoned that, if you poured tea onto the flat cup with enough care, surface tension would hold the liquid in place.

He built a prototype and, after much spilled tea and mopping up, he got the tea to stay in the Flat Cup. He then decided to see if the tea would hold as the Flat Cup was in motion, so walked across the road to show his sister Nancy, also an inventor. (Remember the Flat Cap Torch Holder? That was one of hers.)

Sadly, just as he left the house, balancing the tea very carefully in the Flat Cup, it began to rain. Always being inventive, he put the Flat Cup on his head without losing any of the tea.

So a Flat Cup became, in a strange twist of history, a Flat Cap!

THE FLAT CAP CUT
(elsewhere known as a) Basin Cut

The tale of a tattoo

Steve Bucknell-Toast loved his flat cap. He'd had it since he was fifteen and now, at the age of fifty-six, he wanted to celebrate it in some way.

He thought about having a portrait painted, a photograph done, a sculpture sculpted or a commemorative song recorded by a boy band.

In the end, though, he decided to have a tattoo because, as he said, "My flat cap's really an extension of my body and so I'd like to have some body art." Bit of a philosopher, old Steve.

He went along to the village's last remaining tattoo artist, Shaky Pete. He passed Pete a drawing of the flat cap and the inscription he'd like:

A Flat Cap is Forever

Shaky Pete nodded and set to work. The needle buzzed. Steve sweated and grimaced. After several hours Pete stopped and showed Steve a mirror in triumph. The flat cap was perfect. The slogan, however, read:

A Flat Carp is Forever

Let's draw a veil over the rest of that long, long day.

FLAT CAP ARTIST ALFONSO SHUFFLEBOTTOM AT WORK (1926)

The forgotten board game of Flatcapoly

In 1937 the amateur board-game manufacturer Alice Woolnough, intrigued by the success of the recently invented Monopoly, decided to create what she called "a game fit for us tykes".

Having abandoned a Yorkshire version of draughts called 'By, It's Draughty in Here!' and a Yorkshire version of chess with the King as a mill-owner and the Pawns as toiling wage-slaves, Alice went back to Monopoly, used it as her template and, after several days of toil in her shed, came up with 'Flatcapoly, T' Yorksher Game'.

Sadly, after a fire in her shed caused by Alice nodding off whilst smoking her briar pipe, not much of the prototype survived. But the remaining parts of Flatcapoly show us:

Instead of the boot and the dog, each piece was a flat cap in different colours.

On the GO square it said 'Collect 200 Flat Caps'.

The money was in an odd flat-cap-based currency, from a One Cap to a Five Hundred Cap note.

Instead of going to jail, players had to squat inside a vast flat cap.

Alice later made her fortune with her Yorkshire version of Cluedo, called 'Who's Spilt That Gravy?'

Albert Grimsby won his 100th Yorkshire flat cap playing for Yorkshire against Brazil in 1892

THE HAT OF GOD

(George Tumbly scores a contentious goal for Yorkshire against Argentina in the 1896 world cup final)

Minutes of a marketing meeting at the head offices of Pzazz, Tha Knaws PR company, 23rd March 1998

- AB said that he had been approached by Frost & Sons, flat cap manufacturers of Heckmondtwistle, to, as they said, "drag the cap into the twentieth century".
- BB pointed out that it was almost the end of the twentieth century.
- AB said that was debatable in Heckmondtwistle. Laughter ensued and was minuted.
- AB Welcomed CB and DB from the Creative Team.
- CB took some time to erect his flip chart.
- DB helped CB and was rebuffed.
- AB tapped his watch rhythmically.
- CB and DB began their presentation, entitled 'The Lid'.
- DB explained that the common slang name for the flat cap was 'The Lid' and that henceforth the cap would be known as The Lid.
- CB almost laughed when the flip chart collapsed but retained his composure.

- CB outlined the marketing opportunities: The Lid Skateboards, The Lid Hip Hop Mufflers, The Lid Marmalade.
- AB asked if CB and DB had been drinking.
- CB and DB replied that they had not.
- AB said that he'd lived in Yorkshire all his life and had never ever heard the flat cap referred to as The Lid.
- BB said that he'd lived in Yorkshire all his life and had never ever heard the flat cap referred to as The Lid.
- CB said that he thought he had.
- DB said that he'd definitely heard someone in a market refer to it as The Lid.
- When pressed by AB and BB DB said he couldn't recall the location of the market or the month he'd heard it.
- BB asked if there were any other ideas.
- CB and DB said there were no other ideas.
- The meeting ended at 15.30. AB wanted it minuted that CB and DB had better come up with a better idea quickly or they'd be swinging from the washing line like a pair of pants.

Ten strange flat cap facts

1) Queen Victoria was the first member of the royal family to wear a flat cap. She wore it during an incognito visit to a music-hall show.

2) A flat cap was found by its owner on Scarborough beach thirty years after he dropped it from a cross-channel ferry. The owner described it as 'soggy but wearable.'

3) The Flat Cap Butterfly of Antarctica is so called because its wings resemble a flat cap.

4) The Flat Cap War was fought from 1876 to 1882 between the villages of North Burton and South Burton using only flat caps as weapons; nobody was hurt, although one man got hair cream poisoning.

5) A Flat Cap Chair was designed by Jeremiah Jones of Skipton for his aged mother Jenny to sit in; sadly it collapsed as she sat in it and, frankly, she never forgave him.

6) A Flat Cap-shaped air balloon was seen over the Western Front trenches on Christmas Day 1915. The pilot of the balloon dropped novelty paper flat caps on the soldiers from both sides.

7) A horse called Flat Cap lost more races than any other horse in history apart from one called, oddly, Fedora.

8) There are seventeen houses in the world called Flat Cap, one called My Flat Cap and one called Dun Flat Cappin.

9) The worst ever spelling of Flat Cap was tykd bbl5 by Steve Mason of Rotherham.

10) Flat Cap is a variety of grey on the Glossop's Paints colour chart.

You will be hanged by the....

The Flat Cap Skirmish of 1899

We can laugh about it now through the lens of history, but at the time The Flat Cap Skirmish of 1899 was a very serious matter indeed.

The two villages of Breshington and Brushley-by-the-Brush were separated only by the River Brush (if you lived at one side of the river) and the River Bresh (if you lived at the other side of the river).

Both villages had just one main employer, a flat cap factory. In Breshington it was the Bresh Mill, in Brushley … well, you get the drift.

Queen Victoria was to visit Yorkshire and it was decided that she should be presented with a proper Yorkshire flat cap. John Bruttle of Bresh Mill insisted the cap should come from his establishment and James Brettle of Brush Mill insisted … well, you get the drift.

Both Mills made a prototype Royal Crown/Cap item of hybrid headgear and took it to the bridge across the river to show the mayor of each town. Details of what happened next are sketchy but first voices, then caps, then clenched fists, then items of cap-making machinery were raised in anger. A mêlée ensured which quickly grew into a riot and then into a pitched battle. Shouts of "She'll wear our cap!" and "She knows our cap's fit for a queen!" echoed round the valley.

Sadly, several people were injured, some seriously. Perhaps even more sadly Queen Victoria opted in the end for a muffler from Methley's Mufflers.

But the Flat Cap Skirmish of 1899 remains in the minds of the people of the area, and indeed it was commemorated in the ballad, recorded for the first time in print, opposite:

The Ballad of the Flat Cap Skirmish of 1899

It came to pass
There was a bit of a flap
When the queen had to wear
One of our flat caps

Oh, the Flat Cap Skirmish!
Oh, the Flat Cap Skirmish!

She couldn't decide
Which one to wear
The one from over here
Or the one from over there

Oh, the Flat Cap Skirmish!
Oh, the Flat Cap Skirmish!

And a few blows were struck
And necks were slapped
And heads were thumped
Over t' Queen's flat cap

Oh, the Flat Cap Skirmish!
Oh, the Flat Cap Skirmish!

And blood were spilt
And necks got brock
And the whole place was
In a state of shock

Oh, The Flat Cap Skirmish!
Oh, The Flat Cap Skirmish!

Now peace has come
And calm descends
And the warring folks
Are best of friends

Until the next Flat Cap Skirmish!
The very next Flat Cap Skirmish!

Ten past eleven in the Station Hotel

Jim: Reyt, I'm off in a minute.

Jem: See yer termorrer.

Jim: Nar then: wheer's mi flat cap?

Jem: Ah've not sin it. Good neet!

Jim: Heyop: what's this?

Jem: Good neet! Dun't miss t' last bus!

Jim: What's mi cap doin' under your beer?

Jem: Er…

Jim: Nay! It's all soggy like! It's wringing wet!

Jem: Well I couldn't find me beermat — I had to put summat under.

Jim: Well, I can't wear this ter gu ooam! It's sooakin!

Jem: Tha can! It's rainin'!

Jim: That's all reet then! Good neet!

Jem: Good neet!

I can't describe, they had
their caps pulled down

The short-lived and not-very-succcessful flat-cap-based currency

The small village of Shaftness near Wakefield decided, in 2003, to adopt a currency based entirely upon the Flat Cap. Thousands of coins were minted and a similar number of notes were printed. Shops on the high street altered their prices to fit the new money, so that a loaf of bread was Three Flat Caps and a pint of beer was Five Flat Caps.

Sadly the good burghers of Shaftness hadn't worked out the conversion very deeply; each coin and each note were just worth One Flat Cap. No change could be issued. An instant flat cap inflation took place and people took their wages home in wheelbarrows.

The experiment was not a success and was quickly forgotten.

Until now.

The 3.15 Yorkshire Headgear Handicap

"…and they're coming to the final furlong now with Flat Cap in the lead followed by Big Flat Cap and Floppy Flat Cap and Tiny Flat Cap and Really Old Flat Cap That Should Have Been Chucked Away is a long long way back and on the turn it's Tiny Flat Cap Tiny Flat Cap a neb in front of Flat Cap with Really Old Flat Cap That Should Have Been Chucked Away coming up on the rails…

"And we've got a faller! We've got a faller! Floppy Flat Cap has flapped and flopped and flipped onto the turf and Tiny Flat Cap is coming away from the field now Tiny Flat Cap in the lead from Flat Cap and the rest of the field trailing …

"Apart from Really Old Flat Cap That Should Have Been Chucked Away which is gaining on Flat Cap and Tiny Flat Cap and going faster and faster and making me talk fasterandfaster and say all my words at the same time …

"And it's ReallyOldFlatCapThatShouldHaveBeenChucked Away gaining on FlatCap and TinyFlatCap has fallen and it's a tussle between ReOFlaCaThaShuHaBeChuA and FlaCa…

"And it's a photo! It's a photo finish!

"And my voice is slowing down   now   the   race is   over   so   it's   a   photo between   Tiny Flat   Cap   and   Really   Old   Flat Cap   That   Should   Have   Been Chucked   Away …"

TARZAN T'APE MAN

The Flat Coupé

The Yorkshire car-making firm Snellist was trying to move with the times; we're all familiar with their smooth-but-dull family car the Snellist Snug and their estate model the Snellist Lounge but the Snellist Brothers who ran the firm had a hankering for something, in the words of the younger Snellist, George, 'sexy'. And yes, that's obviously a word they would never have used in front of their late dad Horace.

The older brother Maxwell had an idea for developing a sporty model, something that could get out of third gear very easily and tackle the hills of Hebden Bridge with aplomb, so they designed a flat, aerodynamic speedster that could whizz and zoom and do all the things that fast cars do.

They knew the car would be a success, but they wanted to come up with a name that would reflect the elegance and speed of the vehicle. So they sat with a pot of strong tea and a flipchart, and tried to come up with something that had pizzazz and brio. Indeed, they wrote down the words Pizzazz and Brio as possible names for the new car but decided they looked too much like Pizza and Biro.

After discarding names like the Fast and the Faster, they decided to concentrate on the firm's Yorkshire heritage as a way of generating the name. The Muffler. No good. The Pudding. Worse. The Parkin. An elaborate pun, but still useless. Then Maxwell clicked his fingers and said "The Flat Cap", and almost at the same time George said "The Flat Coupé" — pronounced 'coop'.

And they decided that the name was genius, sheer genius.

And they only ever sold six, so they decided it wasn't.

...and to my favourite son Osbert
I leave my collection of flat caps..

The infamous missed marketing opportunity

In 1973 Wilf Lumsden-Lumb, managing director of the Double L Flat Cap Company of Mastin Street, Heckmondwike, was going for his customary lunchtime walk; he said it helped him to clear his head and think of new advertising and manufacturing opportunities for Double L Flat Caps.

It was an extremely windy day in West Yorkshire and, as Wilf turned Windy Corner, his flat cap (Double L, of course) was lifted from his head and spiralled into the garden of Doris McNou, a member of the local church choir.

Going into the garden to retrieve the cap, Wilf was amazed to notice that it had landed, with some force, on Doris's left foot, wrapping itself around the toes like a glove. Well, a glove on a hand, but you get my drift. Doris commented just how warm the cap was and suggested that he market a special flat cap for feet called a Foot Cap. Sadly, Wilf dismissed the idea out of hand as a bit of Women's Nonsense, picked up his cap and went back to the factory.

Incensed, Doris took her Foot Cap idea to Wilf's rival Trevor 'The Headcovering' Tinsley of Double T caps, and the rest, as they say, is history.

But don't mention it to Wilf; he still walks every lunchtime.

Mention it to Trevor, if you like: he swims every lunchtime in the private pool of his villa in the South Of France. Casa Foot Cap, he calls it.

Breaking news:
Evidence of Cro-Magnon flat caps

Archeologists studying prehistoric cave paintings near Hebden Bridge have come up with a theory that Cro-Magnon people wore primitive versions of flat caps made of flat stones. Images on the walls appear to show people in animal skin with enormous flat surfaces on their heads, a little like mortar boards or, to be frank, bin lids.

One particular painting seems to depict a Cro-Magnon Yorkshireman walking through a storm with the rain bouncing off the flat stone.

The archaeologists are also speculating that the reason so many Yorkshiremen have big fat bulbous necks is a throwback to when the flat cap was granite and weighed a ton.

"I'm very excited about this," said Professor Walt Blenkinsop of Heckmondwike University, "and I'm hoping to try an experiment next week when I try to walk around all day with a flat stone on my head."

His wife was unavailable for comment.

Flat cap acrostics

The *Yorkshire Gent* was a short-lived monthly lifestyle magazine published in Harrogate during the 1920s. As well as features on Yorkshire Pudding Mixing, Knurr and Spell Heroes and Interactive Parkin Sculpture, they ran a popular Flat Cap Acrostics page, where readers would devise Yorkshire-based acrostics around the words 'Flat' and 'Cap'. A prize was awarded each month for the best one. As the editor at the time said:

"These Flat Cap Acrostics contain nuggets of wisdom, the drive of narrative and the glittering language of the best poetry."

Here's a selection. You can judge for yourself …

Fred
Loved
Aysgarth's
Teashop's
Cuppas
And
Pastries

Feeling
Low?
'Aving
Treatment?
Chew
Aniseed
Pastilles!

Five
Long
And
Trembly
Cats
Attacked
Peter

Fly,
Little
Airship,
To
Castleford
And
Pontefract!

Frances
Latimer
Angered
Trevor
Charlesworth
At
Pickering

THE BAYEUX TAPESTRY

Lawrence of the Dales

FLAT CAP SAVES LIFE OF PENSIONER

For years Albert Mottram's wife Alberta had told him to wash his flat cap and for years he'd refused, saying that if he washed it, it would fall apart. Every Sunday, as Albert mixed his Yorkshire puddings, he'd absent-mindedly rub his cap and Yorkshire pudding mix would adhere; then, when he got the lard to put in the tins, he'd absent-mindedly rub his cap and lard would adhere. This meant that over the decades his cap had become shellacked, hardened, plastered. If you flicked it with your finger, it would ring like a lardy bell.

On Sunday last, Albert was walking through Ilkley when a cat belonging to Trudy Stanshall-Otley fell from the bedroom window of her bijou villa on to his head. Due to overfeeding and lack of exercise the cat, Samson, weighed thirteen stones and the impact would have flattened a lesser man or a man whose flat cap had not been preserved and toughened by years of lard and pudding mix. The cat bounced off, unhurt, and Albert strolled on, unhurt.

His wife said "It's a good job he took no notice of me telling him to wash his flat cap," and Albert nodded sagely, which was difficult due to the weight of the cap.

from the archives of the *Ilkley Argus*, 21st March 1934

Flat Cap Wind Scale

Force one: Flat Cap remains calm.

Force two: Flat Cap shifts a little on the head.

Force three: Flat Cap revolves slightly on its axis.

Force four: Flat Cap has to be held on with
one hand.

Force five: Flat Cap has to be held on with
two hands.

Force six: Flat Cap flies from head a distance not
more than ten feet.

Force seven: Flat Cap flies from head at speed a
distance of up to half a mile.

Force eight: Citizens within reach of Flat Caps
should take cover in sturdy buildings
with no windows.

Force nine: All air traffic suspended for fear of
flying Flat Caps.

Force ten: End of known world due to Flat Caps
being blown around.

Cloud formations   No 25...
flatus Capus

Flat cap used as cat flap

George and Bertha Mixenden's cat Cripps always liked to settle down for the night on one of George's old flat caps, the one he wore for the Queen's Coronation in 1953. When George had a cat flap fitted in the front door he found that Cripps wouldn't use it, and indeed seemed slightly frightened of it.

Bertha hit on an ingenious solution: she nailed George's coronation cap on to the front of the cat flap like a door and, as Cripps approached it to snuggle up to it, he fell in or out of it.

And now Cripps sleeps on the flat cap George wore for the visit of the Queen to Halifax in 1956, so everyone is happy.

Flat cap used for Pat slap

Pat Smythe was a bus driver who could never get out of bed for the early shift; he always slept through the alarm, and his wife's shouts and unsubtle rib-nudging.

However, one way of getting him out from between the sheets was to slap him hard with his granddad's old Double-Nebbed Thunderer, a kind of flat cap manufactured in Todmorden between the wars, and much admired for its weight and heft.

As they used to say in Todmorden:

"Tha'll hev a big neck if tha wears one of them for too long."

THE TWO-MAN FLATCAP SLEIGH

Flat cap used as bat map

The intrepid nineteenth-century bat-hunter Tobias Weekes recalled in his memoir *Hanging Upside Down for a Living* how he once accidentally stumbled upon a cave in the Yorkshire Dales that was full of hundreds of different kinds of bats which hadn't been recorded before. He writes:

"… I felt a great sense of consternation that, as the scarce bats flapped around me, I had no notebook in which to write down my observations. However, I was wearing my trusty flat cap, the top of which was covered in bat detritus from previous bat hunts. I was able to scratch a map of the different bat habitats in the cave on the aforementioned bat detritus with my fingernail, thus saving the day."

Flat Cap Island: an ocean mystery

On the 10th October 1963 a ragged-dressed man was found by a passing cargo ship in the middle of the Atlantic Ocean clinging to some spars of wood that had obviously once been a raft. He ranted and raved in what his American rescuers assumed was a hybrid Inuit/Martian language until the ship's cook, a man from Dewsbury, revealed to them that he was speaking Yorkshire dialect.

The cook, one Steve Linshaw from Doncaster, recorded what the man was saying, and transcribed it. I think it's a remarkable and chilling story, although people I've shown it to say it's contrived and ridiculous rubbish. You decide.

(If you wish to read it aloud, then try to imagine Long John Silver as played by a Yorkshireman in an amateur dramatic production.)

"Flat Cap Island! Ah harrr! Flat Cap Island! Ah were shipwrecked, me hearties tha knows, after a grett storm! Ah Harr! I swam to an island and I sat theer on t' beach for a bit gerrin' me breath back, tha knows. Ah Harr! Then I took stock o' me situation, like, an' I noticed that t' island were fairly flat but at one end there were a curvy beach, tha knows. I climbed up to t' middle of t' island which were on a bit of a slight rise, like, and I noticed that t' island were in t' shape on a flat cap wi' that curvy beach thing being t' neb on t' cap. Ah Harr!

"And as tha knows there's allus a little press-stud on t' neb that tha can click to looisen thi cap. And on Flat Cap Island this press-stud were actually a stooan.

"An' I went up to t' stooan an' I noticed a big X on it. An' I thought 'X marks the spot' — there's treasure theer! An' I tried to lift t' stooan burra couldn't! And I knew mi dad had a jemmy in his shed that I could use to get t' stooan up!

"So I medd a raft. And I sailed away from Flat Cap Island. Ah Harr! I sailed away on mi raft to get to mi dad's shed so that ah could get his jemmy and jemmy up t' stooan on t' neb-beach that were on Flat Cap Island! Ah Harr! Ah Harr!! Ah Harr!!!"

Oddly, no-one had ever been able to find Flat Cap Island since …

YORKSHIRE SAYINGS no 16

Eee by gum... it's rainin'
caps and clogs

FOLK SINGER JARVIS PLAYS A CAPJO, AN EARLY YORKSHIRE MUSICAL INSTRUMENT

Memories of Flat Cap Albion

Note: Flat Cap Albion was a hippy commune established in the moors above Tong in 1969. These memoirs (some may call them ramblings) were transcribed from an interview with Peace McFee, a man often described as 'Batley's First Hippy'.

"Yeah, like, we all wore the flat cap, man. The flat cap was like a symbol of the oppression of the working class and a desire to keep your combover in place, but we turned it into a badge of freedom, man, and a shining light of Albion! That's all we wore, man.

"We only wore the flat cap, in all weathers, in all seasons, we only wore the flat cap. It was freezing, man, or we burned our botties off, but we stuck to the cap, man.

"I tried to smoke one, once. I rolled it up, put it in my mouth and set fire to it, man. Set fire to the yurt. Bad vibes.

"Grew things in the cap. Made soup in the cap. Made thistle tea in the cap. Got washed in the cap: it didn't hold much water but that didn't matter because we didn't like getting washed, man!

"Had a dog called Flat Cap. I'd throw the flat cap for Flat Cap and he'd catch it and bring it back. Happy hippy dippy days, man!"

In the flat cap night sky

Young Steven and his granddad
Pointing to the sky
As they stand in the yard.

"See how flat the sky is, Steven lad,
How high the moon is, how high
The stars are." "They look like lard,

Granddad," says Steven, a bit of a poet.
"Bits of lard at the edge of the frying pan
Of the sky." Grandad smiles. "And here's me

thinking they look like a flat cap. I know, it
seems daft and don't tell your gran,
but those stars there could just about be

In the shape of a flat cap." And he was right.
And the flat cap glowed in the Yorkshire night.

The Flat Cap Scene from King Lear
(now lost)

Lear: Oh fool, what dost thou sport upon thy head?
      It seems exceeding flat, and dull, i' faith,
      As Lincolnshire and Norfolk, two flat places in the East.

Fool: Oh sir, I wear a cap whose flatness is the roundness of itself
      And if the world is flat then this cap be too and so
      Because the world is round this cap, this flat cap,
      Cannot be the world and so the flat cap is world unto itself.

Lear: You mean you've lost your trilby?

Fool: I hath.

Don't worry, Moses will be fine

Hello, Guinness Book of Records...

The man in the cap

In 1957 the *Morley Times* instigated a competition to boost circulation called 'Are You the Man in the Cap?'. The idea was that a junior member of staff (usually, though not exclusively, Keith Monk, the gardening correspondent and writer of the Fun With Uncle Keith Kiddies' Kolumn) would don a huge flat cap and walk round small towns and villages in the Morley area until a reader, armed with a copy of the *Morley Times*, would challenge him and say "You are the Man in the Cap", and Keith would give the winner a ten-shilling note. (A special ten-shilling note which could only be exchanged for copies of the *Morley Times*.)

Sadly the scheme went disastrously wrong because most of the citizens, both male and female, of West Yorkshire, wear huge flat caps all the time, winter and summer. Innocent people would be accosted by other innocent people who spouted the slogan and were eager for their ten-bob note. Arguments, fights, slappings, scrums and mini-riots occurred as Keith Monk sat in a kafé having koffee and kake.

The scheme was quietly dropped.

The Globetrotting cap

May 1962: George Dawson emigrates to Australia, takes his favourite flat cap with him.

July 1971: George's wife, unknown to George, takes his cap to a charity shop in Canberra.

August 1971: Sam McGee buys the cap from the shop. He likes to wear it when he's gardening.

September 1976: Sam McGee goes on a world cruise and takes his charity shop flat cap to shield him from the Sun.

October 1976: The cap is blown from Sam's head during a bad storm just off the coast of Brazil. It floats for months, occasionally sinking, occasionally coming to the surface.

December 1976: The cap is picked up by a passing gannet and dropped onto the deck of a cargo ship, where it rolls behind a funnel.

February 1977: The cargo ship docks in Canberra. A cleaner chucks the cap over the side of the boat, where it lands on the head of George Dawson, who is taking his dog for a walk.

How was Australia?

Aren't tha goin't take tha cap off first?

Flat cap skimming

The game of flat cap skimming across the River Dearne is celebrated each year by the people of Goldthorpe, near Barnsley.

The tradition began in the 1920s when a group of miners were trying to encourage their children to skim stones across the water. One particular lad called Albert Ainscough just couldn't seem to grasp the technique, so his dad Percy pulled the flat cap from his head and skimmed it. It bounced twenty times before landing on the far bank. Percy and Albert's mates were amazed, and they all had to have a go.

Flat cap skimming reached a peak in the years between the wars but fell into sharp decline in the 1950s after a number of injuries caused by people trying to skim themselves across the water while wearing their flat caps.

Folklorists are currently trying to revive the tradition, so if you're ever near the River Dearne in Goldthorpe do have a go.

THE EROTIC DANCE of the FLAT CAP
(drives men barmy)

Rules for wafting soup in a posh café with your flat cap

Always ask first; some of the posher cafés have wafting implements to hand, some of the really posh cafés employ wafters, some do not allow wafting at all.

Do not waft quickly; this can cause a side-wind which can annoy or gravely injure fellow-diners.

Do not sing the old 'Wafty Wafty' song, particularly the second verse as this may cause offence, particularly to diners called Horace

Make sure your sleeves do not dangle in the soup as you waft; this can cause the bowl to tip over and pour soup into your flat cap.

Remember to hold on tight: flat caps can be dropped into the soup if you're not careful.

On no account use two flat caps to waft your wife's soup as well as your own. She will not be impressed, indeed she may well tut and roll her eyes.

Happy wafting!

Words buried in a time capsule alongside a flat cap

Not To Be Opened Before 2113

Greetings, People of t' Future from People of t' Present!

We are from Yorkshire, the capital of the world.

We have buried in this time capsule a Flat Cap, otherwise known as the Yorkshire Crown.

Wear it and you will be a king anywhere you go.

People will assume you are of high parentage.

People will shower you with gifts.

People will bow their knees in obeisance.

People will want to kiss your hand.

Wear this cap always, even in bed, for it has magical powers.

Yours, in the Fellowship of the Flat Cap,
the People of t' Present
(who, by the time you read this,
will the People of t' Past)

His last wish was to be buried in a flat cap

t' exterminate!
t' exterminate!

UFOS HAD 'SIMPLE EXPLANATION'

A number of sightings of Unidentified Flying Objects over Malton Market Square last week were today identified as merely flat caps thrown in the air by members of the local darts team celebrating a win over local rivals Pickering.

"It's summat we allus do, like," said the team captain Josiah Thackray. "When we've betten Pick, we chuck us caps in t' air. We try an chuck 'em up as far as we can, an' some of 'em can appear to be somewheeer near t' stratosphere, like."

Police said they'd been inundated with reports of flat-cap-like objects in the sky.

"We didn't realise they were flat caps," said an officer from the Police Intelligence Unit.

From the *Malton Observer*, 7th May 1952

Overheard in the Gardeners Arms

"I didn't have the heart to move it, like. That blackbird had built a nest in my cap. Took her time doing it, an' all, carrying twigs an' bits of straw from all over the place. Had three eggs, sat on 'em for ages, then hatched out three lovely chicks, chirruping beautiful. Where was the cap? On my head, of course. I'm wearing it now, look…"

Yorkshire entry for the
1976 Eurovision Song Contest

OOO I Like my flat cap!
Do you like my flat cap?
I really like your flat cap!
Why don't we get together?

OOO It's a practical thing is a flat cap!
And a lovely object is a flat cap!
And a work of art is a flat cap!
And it keeps out t'Yorkshire weather!

It's flatter than a pancake
Or a still still pond
And when I wear mine
I feel like James Bond!

You can get 'em in all colours
Well, from brown to green
And when I wear mine
I feel like a love machine!

OOO I like my flat cap!
Do you like my flat cap?
I really like your flat cap!
Why don't we get together?

Repeat and fade.

(Null points, by the way.)

Flat cap variations that never caught on

Flat Cup: "It's the cup that's as flat as a saucer!" as the 1950s advertising jingle went.

Flat Carp: an attempted hybrid of a carp and a flatfish, never bred successfully in captivity.

Flat Clap: A method of applause created by flapping the hands together back to front, creating a muffled or 'flat' sound. Never popular.

Flit Cap: A huge flat cap on wheels that doubled as a removal van. Never got past the prototype stage.

Flight cap: Flat Cap with wings attached, "for the busy Northern commuter". Never available to the consumer after trials in high wind.

Flute Cap: A flat cap that you could play through a mouthpiece. Discontinued after it was discovered that all the notes were flat.

Fleet Cap: Combination flat cap and sailor's cap, used only in the short-lived Staithes Independent Navy (1906-7).

Float Cap: Flat cap used as rescue device in the aforementioned Staithes Independent Navy.

That's him, I recognise the hat

THE FLAT CAP DEPRESSION OF 1933

ROTHERHAM MAN ATTEMPTS TO CROSS CHANNEL IN FLAT CAP

Rotherham bus driver Phil 'I'm Daft' Bluther will this evening attempt to cross the English Channel in a specially strengthened and elongated flat cap.

The cap, which belonged to his Uncle George, was stretched on a rack for three months and then laminated with a mixture of yacht varnish and gaffer tape.

When asked if he's worried about his attempt he replied:

"No, I'm daft!"

Mr. Bluther has made previous unsuccessful attempts to cross the channel in a Yorkshire Pudding and a Giant Curd Tart.

Rotherham Advertiser, 7th June 1998

3 MEN IN A FLAT CAP

THE YORKSHIRE 10 COMMANDMENTS

...' an' tha must not covet
t'neighbour's flat cap...

Bill Totley's 1973 Christmas hit
Me Flat Cap's Too Fat

I can't get down the chimney
'cos me flat cap's too fat
Me flat cap's too fat
And I'm stuck
And all the little kiddies wanting presents and that
Are out of Christmas luck!

Chorus:
Oh Santa is from Yorkshire
And his flat cap
Keeps his head warm
Oh Santa's got a flat cap
And Rudolph's got one too!

But I can't get down the chimney
'cos me flat cap doesn't fit me
It doesn't fit me
And the chimney's tight
And all the little kiddies will be out of luck tonight...

Repeat Chorus

(Highest position in charts: 4,532)

HMH

(his master's hat)

THE FAB FOUR FLAT CAPS

She loves puds yeah yeah yeah
she loves puds yeah...

Oh Me Old Flat Cap*

Oh me old flat cap
Is flatter than me head
flatter than a pancake
flatter than a bed
Oh me old flat cap
Is the flattest thing around
But because I've wasted all this time singing
I've dropped a number of valuable peas on the
Unforgiving ground.**

*traditional nineteenth-century pea-picking song
**scholars believe that the last three lines were imposed on the song by APF (Association of Pea Farmers)

Flat-cap-related local newspaper headlines

MAN LIVED FOR THREE YEARS ON DIET OF FLAT CAPS

FLAT-CAP-SHAPED OBJECT NOT UFO, SAY BOFFINS

FLAT CAP THIEF APPREHENDED: 4,000 IN HIS FLAT

"I'M NO FLAT CAP" SAYS PETE

MARKS ON INSIDE OF FLAT CAP LOOK LIKE HENRY 8TH!

FLAT CAP FOUND ON MOON

"I'M A FLAT CAP" SAYS PETE

FLAT CAP FEATURES IN NEW JAMES BOND FILM

"WEARING A FLAT CAP KEEPS ME YOUNG" SAYS 100-YEAR-OLD MAN

FAMILY DISPUTE OVER WHO INHERITS 100-YEAR-OLD FLAT CAP

speed trap cap

THE BARNSLEY BIG HATS

Yorkshire pub names

The Flat Cap

T' Flat Cap

The Flattest Cap

The Dog and Cap

The Cap and Duck

The King's Cap

The Queen's Cap

The Brewery Cap

The Cap and Spile

The Ring Round the Head

See if you can have a pint in them all!

Notes of experiment by Professor Obadiah Wetfish of Whitby University to study flat cap through a microscope

Fabric almost destroyed by decades of wear.

Evidence of chip fat from keeping chips warm in cap.

Evidence of soup from attempting to keep soup in cap.

Evidence of ageing of wearer as traces of hair go from black to grey. Also evidence of hair restoration cream.

Evidence of barbed wire from months cap spent hanging from barbed wire fence.

Evidence of beer stains from years spent mopping beer up at the Dog and Duck after shove ha'penny disputes.

Flat-cap-beetle eggs very much in evidence.

Uncle Charlie's caps

Uncle Charlie had three flat caps:
Pit
Garden
Best.

And when he died my Auntie
Left them where they were:
Pit
Garden
Best.

A reminder of the man who wore them
And only rarely took them off:

Pit
Garden
Best.

Flat symbols of who he was.